# KISSING A BONE

MAURA DOOLEY

# Kissing a Bone

BLOODAXE BOOKS

ISBN: 1 85224 373 2

First published 1996 by
Bloodaxe Books Ltd,
P.O. Box 1SN,
Newcastle upon Tyne NE99 1SN.

Bloodaxe Books Ltd acknowledges
the financial assistance of Northern Arts.

Cover printing by J. Thomson Colour Printers Ltd, Glasgow.

Printed in Great Britain by
Cromwell Press Ltd, Broughton Gifford, Melksham, Wiltshire.

*for my father*

Your heart, like an old milk tooth
hanging by a thread: a strength we'd test
with temper, trust, the exquisite tug of truth.

*Enlarged*, we knew what that meant.

And now, I want your big heart here,
to chart its absences: the yellow stream
of bitterness, the silver river of malice,
the empty shore of Lake Envy,

all the landscapes it had never known
and all the different countries it contained.

# Acknowledgements

Acknowledgements are due to the editors of the following publications in which some of these poems first appeared: *Agenda*, *Blade*, *Bound Spiral*, *British Council New Writing 2* & *3* (Minerva, 1993 & 1994), *British Council New Writing 5* (Vintage, 1996), *The Guardian*, *Independent on Sunday*, *The Long Pale Corridor: contemporary poems of bereavement* (Bloodaxe Books, 1996), *New Welsh Review*, *The North*, *Oxford Magazine*, *Poetry Book Society Anthology* (PBS/Hutchinson, 1991), *Poetry with an Edge* (Bloodaxe Books, revised edition, 1993), *PPQ*, *Sixty Women Poets* (Bloodaxe Books, 1993), *Slow Dancer*, *Soundings*, *Southern Review* (USA), *Stopping for Death: poems of death and loss* (Viking, 1996), and *Verse*.

Some poems were broadcast on *Young Poets* and *Night Waves* (BBC Radio 3) and on *Word of Mouth* (Radio 4). '1847' won third prize in the National Poetry Competition in 1994.

'Does It Go Like This' was commissioned for the Hay-on-Wye Squantum in 1992. 'Echolalia' was commissioned by Age Concern/ Southern Arts Board in 1994. 'Home' was commissioned by the Crafts Council of Ireland/Midlands Arts Centre for the exhibition *Words Revealed* in 1996.

I am very grateful to London Arts Board for a New Writing Award given in 1994.

# Contents

## History

It's only a week but already you are slipping
down the cold black chute of history. Postcards.
Phonecalls. It's like never having seen the Wall,
except in pieces on the dusty shelves of friends.

Once I queued for hours to see the moon in a box
inside a museum, so wild it should have been kept
in a zoo at least but there it was, unremarkable,
a pile of dirt some god had shaken down.

I wait for your letters now: a fleet of strange cargo
with news of changing borders, a heart's small
journeys. They're like the relics of a saint.
Opening the dry white papers is kissing a bone.

# Protagonist

He rehearses the station: knows the release
of a brake's steady application,
sweat, anticipation's dying fall,
the mercy of a busy platform,
shadows scattering in the ticket hall,
then the one shadow.

From a window open to the sea,
a town's dark underlife is undertow,
its evening rope of stars and strangers,
hauls him in, silvery, slow, down

down, till he's shown how and where
the thing they've kept hidden,
too sophisticated now even to tick,
might explode into life, or worse,
that other trick. He never meant to do harm,
wanted only to keep their hearts warm.

# Going the Distance

He fills her glass. She raises it.
The nearest he comes to telling her
is here in this silence. With the weight
of his life backed up behind him like a truck,
in the time it takes her heart to skip a beat,
he travels the length of that old road again.

The dream of leaving: nipping out for fags,
a box of matches, never looking back.
Returning to the island after years away
only the coinage would feel strange to him,
crenulations beaten smooth by distance,
shifting in his hand like the sea, whose dazed
blue space, calm and flat beneath him, is
the Atlantic's slow unfurling of its flag.

She drains her glass and lowers it.
The waiter clearing dishes from the table
is tender and efficient as a priest.
They settle up. She opens a door on London.
He closes it. They move into the crowd.

# The Message

How, at an open window the wind
filled a shirt with the shape of his body,
pressed it flat as an idea again.

Then, turning back the covers one still night
she found a bat in her bed, cupped it,
flung its small warmth into the sky.

But, the need for a cigarette
was the need to press hard on the wheel
of his Zippo: pain, ignition.

So, when the parcel came she wasn't surprised
that all his curls spilled out,
clipped, abundant and with no message.
Somewhere, his head was cool and clear and free.

# Heat

Summer swells like a fruit.
Long evenings hang
the way small insects hug a storm lantern.
Already we have forgotten about covers,
know that this will be called *that summer*.

Staring across fields to where
water breaks this land in two
we cannot see it gleaming,
even under full moon.
Intention and purpose
are hidden among long grasses,
the low coughs of sleeping beasts.

How to peel the truth from this,
expose the ripeness of the moment,
juice in our mouths and our hands still clean.

# Faith

When I tell him
that one of my legs
is shorter than the other,

he wants to see
my crooked hips
and discuss provenance.

Instead, we walk in mud
so he can measure depth,
trace the pattern I trail,

mark the constraints of balance,
the imprint of my imperfection
and believe in me.

## Does It Go Like This?

The day seawater swilled my lungs
he guided me back without ever once touching me.
Lying on shingle, like the two halves
of the equator, I thought my heart would burst,

not knowing in which element it drowned.
Now, two hundred miles from him, beached
on larkspur, lark song, I struggle to remember
something I used to know: *did it go like this? Like that?*

*How did it start?* At Capel-y-Ffin what rises
from dark red dirt, what's netted now
is flotsam of sheepskull filleted by maggots,
a dead pony's ribs taut as ships' rigging

and here, where a draught of summer
rinses tired skin with cuckoo syncopation,
with percussion of bees, old fears rush in
fierce as a tide. Blood, not birdsong

pulses at my ear: the strong cross-currents
that beat in these shallows, the meat
and bone under bright meadow grasses,
the heart's tricky business of staying alive.

Remember the day we saw divers trawl the Thames
heavy with rosaries of gas and rope,
angels with black rubber wings and serious faces
dropping through mist and into the deep, like psalms?

What is that tune whose words I try to catch
*Does it go like this? Like this? How does it begin?*
I dredge up only the middle, a jaded chorus,
of a song I used to know right through by heart.

## Up on the Roof

You wonder why it is they write of it, sing of it,
till suddenly you're there, nearest you can get
to flying or jumping and you're alone, at last,
the air bright. Remembering this, I go
with my too-light jacket up to the sixth floor,
out onto the roof and I freeze under the stars
till he comes with my too-heavy jacket, heavier
and heavier, as he tries to muffle my foolishness.
*A blanket on a fire* (he says) and it's true
I am left black, bruised a little, smouldering.

You can sit with a book up there and reel in
life with someone else's bait. You can let your eyes
skim the river, bridges, banks, a seagull's parabola.
At night, you can watch the sky, those strange galaxies
like so many cracks in the ceiling spilling secrets
from the flat above. You can breathe. You can dream.

But he turns to me, as you'd coax a child
in the back of a stuffy car: *we could play I-Spy?*
I look at the black and blue above and the only
letter I find is 'S'. I cannot name
the dust of starlight, the pinheaded planets,
but I can join the dots to make a farming tool,
the belt of a god: all any of us needs is work,
mystery, a little time alone up on the roof.

# THE FUTURE MEMORY

'It's a poor sort of memory that only works
backwards', the Queen remarked.

LEWIS CARROLL: *Alice Through the Looking Glass*

I began to perceive death in the most mundane
of circumstances. Being photographed felt like
being shot: it still does.

JODIE FOSTER

       This is the use of memory:
For liberation – not less of love but expanding
Of love beyond desire, and so liberation
From the future as well as the past.

T.S. ELIOT: *Little Gidding*

# Net and River

The old bus, nose to the road like a dog,
takes them all the way to the village
with its one shop and shining river.

The net she picks is green, uncertain
on its skinny pole as she dips it
back and forth, between the weeds,
over the stones and catches a fish.

A fish. A flicker and jump in water,
in air: a flash like memory itself.

Watching its ugly gasp for life,
the river fall from its back in tears,
the unkind swat of its head on stone,
she has to drop it back again

and let the waters close, the ripples spread
wide and wider till they can't be seen,
till the lip of deepest water stops its trembling.

# Transubstantiation

Is the residue of the person transferred then,
transfixed by rays of the sun?

*The camera steals the soul.*

She'd like to think that whiteness
in the picture's grain's some essence
flit from darkness. That he'd be there,
embossed on light like the host she'd swallow
in the days when she could swallow it.

*Eat me! Drink me!* to be small again,
untroubled by the easy miracle of that word,
not hearing the shutter close against the light.

# Wonderland

'Down, down, down. Would the fall
never *come to an end?*'

LEWIS CARROLL

The dark cloth in his hands,
then over his head, his
own breath warm about him.

She in a box: shadow and light
and like no trapped thing,
bumping at the frame, blind,

but solemn, her seven years
above ground childishly bright
and only her sleep to be plundered.

# Shot

I stand on the grid and wait.
He says they'll turn the air vent on,
just think of something sad,
then something funny.
That napalmed child running,
the day Mr President got killed,
Woody Allen's trial...I say
but Geez, they haven't happened yet.

He wants to have it look authentic.
He needs some shake, tremble, desire.
I say this is not a problem,
this is the very opposite of a problem.
I throw back my head, they turn on the fan,
we do it, we make it, we shoot.

# Stills

The room is a well of silence.
Mirrors are turned to the wall,
in case the soul, barbed like a fish,
should slip unseen under the silver
trapped forever on its final journey.

*He has all of your shades in this box*
was the Chief's cry: and we're to believe,
so Frazer tells us, that those simple – yes –
souls scrambled, fearful, their scattering
an anthropological pattern on a glass plate.

Here's one for the hacks.
Romance, set down in black and white
in which you cannot smell his halitosis,
nor feel the blemish of her temper:
an air-brush clears up pits and pocks.

In this, *Last of her Tribe*,
the Clearances are a jagged emptiness
in her face. Roosevelt records her end
even as he orders it. Prescience.
Call her *last* and she will be.

Focus, block, crop, the sacred red lamp,
the dark, dark room. This is the murdered boy
and this the missing girl. Here is the pool
in which the young man gazed, silver,
so still, you can no longer hear the echo.

# Echolalia

His version, his vision,
of the way the world works
is like those lightning moments
when a voice, a face, a street corner
from thirty years ago suddenly recurs,
raw as a cut. You wonder then
if the view is still the same,
the sun just clearing the chimneys
and the oak shape-shifting
all the long afternoon, and you know
that it can't be, will always be,
forgetting, for that instant,
which end of the telescope
you're looking through.

\*   \*   \*

# Dark

I lit up only slowly,
coming back to life when
it was clear you could not.
My veins thick as cords,
my skin paler. In the year
I grew old my heart rustled,
thin as cigarette paper.

But one of us had to get
warm again. I partied, I fucked,
I lay awake through the smallest
hours watching headlamps sweep
the ceiling like hands of a clock.

You told me how at night they stable
the trains, leaving them snug
in the long tunnels.
So, tell me what they dream of,
humble there, in the dark.

# Blood

*(for Simon Dennis)*

Something leaked into his blood
the way he entered mine
and never left. Old friendship,
where love leaves its watermark
under the years and all
the *keep meaning to*s fall away
to reveal a life maybe you knew,
maybe you didn't, a voice
saying something, a hand,
his, mine,
and how it was taken.

## In the Glass

You make the French sound *u*
to form a perfect cupid's bow. That printed *o*
on tissue's a shade she'd never wear
but suddenly she's there, staring back at you.

How they fill the room, the Dead.
This favourite cup, that heavy chair,
the watercolour you were made to keep
*to remember her by*, she said. You weep.

They run to catch you, sprightly now,
you falter when a familiar phrase
you'd forgotten you knew, forgotten was theirs,
trips off your tongue, *it'll end in tears*.

And here in the glass, that unalterable fact –
your lipstick drying as your eyes grow moist,
her words imprinting caution on your voice –
you knew, there never really was a choice.

# The Captain's Inventory

There were rooms he never entered:
study, living room,

this one, facing south, where the swallows'
return is a gift of purity, measure, hope.
Or the cellar, locked against memory,
tools and turps, earth and darkness.

The kitchen shrank to a toaster and
down through the mansion of his heart
you could hear the echo of feet, slamming
of doors, till everything slowed to this:
chair, bottle, view of the harbour.

# The Celestial Announcer

On the day that you hear
the station announcer
call out the towns and villages
of your life, as if she'd read
the very chapters of your soul,
that knowing way she has of saying *Halifax*,
the way she skirts around poor rainy *Manchester*,
and jumps to the conclusion now of *Luddenden* –
with its ghost of a station
and dream of Branwell drunk under the stars –
and all the big and little places
you have ever been, would like to go,
chanted, charted,

well, then you realise it's time to change
your mind, ticket, journey,
point of departure,
Estimated Time of Arrival
and know that she will lend you wings
for those golden slippers, milk and honey,
bread, roses and a brand new map.

# Dancing at Oakmead Road

Sometimes I think of its bright cramped spaces,
the child who grew there and the one we lost,
how when we swept up for its newest lover
the empty rooms were still so full of us.

The honeyed boards I knew would yet hold close
our dusts, some silver from my father's head,
the resin of the wood would somehow catch
in patina the pattern of his tread.

That time in the back room, laughing and drunk,
Geraldo and his orchestra, a tune
that had you up and waltzing and me quiet,
my throat so achey at the sight of you,

glimpsing for a second how it might have been
before his mouth went down on yours, before
the War, before the children broke into
the dance, before the yoke of work. Before.

# Gone

You were only a bag of soft stuff
but I imagined you like a nut,
your brain beginning to pack itself
around the kernel that is me.
My limpet, my leech,
my little sucker-in of blood.
Gone. Sometimes I think we know
of nothing else, lost loves, lost lives,
the hopeless benediction of rain.

## Metamorphoses

All changed. He shows me a diagram.
It's like third form biology.
A ram's head, a racing bike's drophandles,
detains an inmate for whom my ribs
will bend their bars,
swan, tiger, snake, daughter.

Ah, Phletes, if I can only hold on long enough
to let her slip my bounds and be free.

# Freight

I am the ship in which you sail,
little dancing bones,
your passage between the dream
and the waking dream,
your sieve, your pea-green boat.
I'll pay whatever toll your ferry needs.
And you, whose history's already charted
in a rope of cells, be tender to
those other unnamed vessels
who will surprise you one day,
tug-tugging, irresistible,
and float you out beyond your depth,
where you'll look down, puzzled, amazed.

## Biting Point

In a borrowed car I am following instruction.
*Reverse the car around this corner and pull up*
*safely.* It is uphill, uneven, blind,
the road is busy. I look back. I move slowly.
I look back. Under my baggy shirt
another person stirs, shrugging my skin
like too many bedclothes, impatient.

*In a moment I am going to say* **stop**
*and I want you to stop, under full control,*
*as if in emergency.* My feet stamp the floor.
My daughter bangs crossly. *Stop.*
I have stopped. I have looked-back.
I have looked hard in the mirror.
The car hasn't even stirred the gravel.

*Good*, says my examiner, *I shan't ask you to do that again.*
Outside a Birch lets go of leaves,
I think of my girl and me, each in our carriage,
like Russian dolls. *Drive on*,
the stranger's voice commands. And we do.

## Into Holes

When she was born they gave us
a pair of old sheets
to cut up and sew for the cot.
Gone into holes and golden,
where their bodies' heat had broken
to sweat, the end of sweat, raggedy
where the washing, lying, washing,
wore them and wore them again.

Now that a torn sheet's too wide
for the narrow beds they keep,
and the weight of a loved one's breath
suddenly too much to bear,
I cannot take a scissors
to this, the map of their happiness
where the hushing, laughing, hushing,
warmed us and warms us again.

## Foreign Correspondent

We are inventing for ourselves a story.
The other life. A narrative that frets and stumbles
yet moves along at such a pace, I'm winded.

Water keeps the distance words try to close.

A peace-keeping force means soldiers in,
then soldiers out. The arms embargo's off.
A meteor falls, another sign to read.

I do, I read and read, your words, the heavens'.

Remember, this is the oldest of games:
paper, scissors, stone,
the power of hands pretending.

# The True Ark

If you joined them,
the pieces of the true ark
would make a fleet,
their sails a white road
from here to the horizon.

Stepping from boat to boat,
a frog among waterlilies,
you might peer below deck
and that sharp stink rising
would reveal the lair of
dodo or phoenix or sphinx.

At night, becalmed, you wonder
at the voice calling 'Time!'
as the sails come down and the vessels
break up before your very eyes,
lodging themselves in museums, stories,
as a splinter in your waiting palm.

## Talks About Talks

There's memory, there's truth
and there's the way the machine works:
a splice, a little oil,
a steady hand with the two wires.
I could find a story in it for you,
though it would beggar belief
and you'd hate the ending, or feel
you'd heard it before, it being
not new but one of the six tales
that roam the world in search of a teller.

There's future, there's past
and there's politics:
a speech, a little gossip,
a shakey hand obeying a shaking head.
I could find meaning in it for you,
though it mightn't ring true
and you'd hate the translation, or feel
you'd do better yourself
with a bulky dictionary and body language.

There's talk, there's silence
and there's the way you sit now:
a table, a little fidgeting,
the steady ticking of an old, sad clock.
I could find history in it for you,
though it mightn't be news
and you'd hate the film version, or feel
you'd lived it already, if only
you could remember when and where and why.

# Making Tea in the Corridors of Power

We all knew that disease idled in the water tank
but only she could say who favoured a Hobnob
and from whom the Nice biscuits were hidden.

Turner's was black with very little sugar
but Bates wanted lightener *swirled like a cloud.*
No sweeteners. No sweeteners of any kind.

Bailey's came in a china cup:
the spoon's *tinkle, tinkle* pleasured him,
the vibration, the promise.

After late meetings there was a shuffle, a scuttle
over stale crumbs and in the mornings she could
smell them. Once, she even glimpsed a scaley tail.

## Miss Muffet

It was the howler monkey who scared me
not the stupid spider.

Scraping up his shit I had to use
my good black gloves like shovels.
Imagine his stench in my nostrils,
his slime at my feet, his shriek in my ears!

Let me tell you, I had to fix my thoughts
on breakfast and not mind
history getting it all wrong again.

# 1847

Ma's face is black with hair
her hands are paws.
She does not know me anymore.

Nights toss us cruelly.
Afraid I'll no more wake
I sit stony.

What knots my belly now's
not hunger. Anger.

In Liverpool ships gob us up.
We rot, we scatter.
The quays are maggoty with us.
We do not matter.

## Moss

Your grandmother's castle is
a black and white photograph curling
in the hand's heat, a ruined tower
in the stranger's field. And on the door
your initials, carved in the heart of youth
are not even a speck in the picture's grain.

I'll go there someday. Pull back the barbed wire,
or set the chairs tumbling in the landlord's house
like some technicolored scene from *The Quiet Man*,
tossing my hair like a heritage, accent all wrong.

I'll go there someday find the approach too hard,
the bramble thick and high, the road unmarked,
the tower so softened by moss it's vanished utterly
slipped back into the land, like the language you left.

# Crossmaglen

Finger on catch: rifle – radio –
my job's to follow headlamps cut a track
and if they stop, I start. Rabbits.

From here I cannot see their tremble,
was never close enough to smell the fear.

Long nights I've sewn the pelts together,
slept under cover of their empty skins,
the ticking of those hearts is history.

# SUBURBAN MYTHS

Each sucked a secret, and each wore a mask.

GEORGE MEREDITH: *Modern Love*

# The Line

A heavy linen cloth,
her dress of shooting stars,
the brittle blue of spring,
his sodden woollen shirt.

The peg becomes a pen,
fills the line with cursive,
a changing word in wind,
*love* or *duty* or *life*.

## Of Gaze

Far from home,
released into a new skin,
he remembers himself.

Forgetting how easily he is burnt
he takes off his shirt:
a mole, a vaccination scar,
a twist of dark hair.

A withheld look,
the idea of a fingertip,
the dream of gaze.

# Knowledge

She put down the cup.
A bead of water caught
beneath the rim and fizzed.
She heard but didn't smile
and then he knew.
That other time, the long
midnight walk, her hand
slipped in and out of his
like something wild, all animal.
Now, she put down her cup,
sat like a stone,
heard, saw and didn't smile.

## Battersea Dogs Home

It was when Diana got stuffed
for nuisance calls that he remembered
a voice asking for the scrap yard.

How could he not have known it sooner,
descrambled those codes, laid down
in him like the National Grid?

Finger on the button, ear to the receiver,
hand on my heart, I never knew.
I never knew it was you.

## The Spoils

But when it came to records
I just said *take the lot*.
They're like a map of where
it all went wrong, *tender*, *true*,
the long and winding road.
Not much on anger till I saw
her hold the hammer, remembered
Ella, Bessie, Billie, *sad*, *blue*.

## His Then Wife

The time I saw him at the Services
I thought he looked familiar,
the middle-distance in his eye,
the complicated walk.
You love a man for seven years
(you think you do) but
seven more and it's not the beard,
the grey, the unlikely hat,
that fox you. It's your own name,
tight as your coat, that means
you can't remember his.

# Home

The past
as night is,
pitch, peat,
as blood is
when the heart stops.

* * *

# What Every Woman Should Carry

My mother gave me the prayer to Saint Theresa.
I added a used tube ticket, kleenex,
several Polo mints (furry), a tampon, pesetas,
a florin. Not wishing to be presumptuous,
not trusting you either, a pack of 3.
I have a pen. There is space for my guardian
angel, she has to fold her wings. Passport.
A key. Anguish, at what I said/didn't say
when once you needed/didn't need me. Anadin.
A credit card. His face the last time,
my impatience, my useless youth.
That empty sack, my heart. A box of matches.

## The Discovery

I am the man who discovered Australia,
at 12 noon, one late Indian summer.
Thumbing through my atlas for the farthest
outpost of the known universe
what stopped me was that glorious shape,
I entered there. The coral reefs,
the wide interior, that harbour
with the soaring wings of song:
I was the man who woke to find himself
on the bridge of a violin,
music in his ears, vibration, unholy joy.

# Night Driving

Across the Pennines maybe, at first frost,
when your headlamps make milky the way ahead,

or approaching Toronto at 4.00 a.m.
when stars lie scattered on the still lake,

driving fast, the windows pulled down,
to let the night winds steady your hands

you're tuned into strange stations
playing old hits you wish you didn't know.

Turning a dial fills the air with static:
oceans, the blueness of night

and you own the road, the country.
The radio speaks only to you.

# Keith Jarrett

Riding that piano as if he's fused somehow,
as if the beast of it rising under his hands
might toss him into the air,

its shimmying flank, its hungry mouth,
that tender moment of patience or trickery
before the heels, horns and meat of it

rear into his ears, nose, mouth
and he sings, hums, stamps,
he whispers, pleads, croons,

reining in, easing, taming finally
the wail of the earth, the song of sex,
the long salt sigh in each of us.

# KLM 468 / Dep. Rotterdam 10.45, Arr. London 10.45

A short flight. My plane lifts into cloud.
The cool green rectangles, the dykes,
the glassy city, vanish into vapour.

Arriving at the very moment of departure,
we make the world tick into place again:
a golden revolution in the hands of a watch,

a slow steep descent in white light
like all the snow he tells me never fell,
not a single flake, this strange, unsettling winter.

Below, London's bridges smooth out creases
in a more familiar map. The pilot explains local time,
the change in temperature, variable conditions.

## More Than Twice the Speed of Sound

Some, remembering other blasts, threw themselves
to the ground. Sheep ran in fear and angry farmers
later said they lost their young that day but our small faces,
turned upwards to the bright, white, empty sky,
were wordless, only the baby jiggling in her pram,
bonneted, cosseted, spoke for us all: *again, 'gain, 'gain.*
Windows shattered, glass sprayed like a fountain, splinters
splashing and rolling, rolling to far corners, where today
they surface sometimes between Desirées and King Edwards.

If I could gather them up, each sharp and dangerous fragment,
and piece it all together, make a grouting of my love,
if I could find in it a vivid, extravagant story,
new-ancient like the frescoes of Ravenna,
if I could restore each grimy window-pane, would you,
could you, see it all differently, our wondering faces,
the sound barrier simply waiting to be broken?

# The Bridge

In Africa, under the dark impossible
bridge that links before the War with after,
he gathered the fallen avocado
for squadron leaders who remembered
pyramids of unblemished flesh in Fortnums.

Black and blue, purple as cardinals,
later he carried them back
from occasional trips to London,
his thumb pressing a rough skin, for give,

making up rules for a spell
in the airing cupboard, or nestling
in a bowl of rosy apples. Delicious bruise,
stone-hearted, leathery ark of dreams.

Now, when even the corner shop
displays the burnished fruit,
his memory of war, distant, green,
begins to turn darker and ripen.

# Last Hours in the City

The yellow trams glide past like stray cartoons,
carriage by carriage stripe the street with a story.

On Kruisstraat the man in the blue anorak
tests words on us that the wind cuts up.

Maybe he offers religion or needs money
but all night rain erases his shadow,

and all the other shadows of trains or stories
that polish the tramline's reading of this city.

In the morning, through his open window,
traffic noise will ripen like a field of wheat,

the falling weight of afternoon recalling
prairies, home, a golden square before him,

no shade anywhere, then dusk again,
like hunger, eating into night.

## Pathetic Magic

At the door
the love we want to offer
gathers itself.

*Safe Home, Take Care,*
*Good Luck, God Bless,*
a rabbit's foot.

Nothing saves us
from the boat tossed over,
a leaf in storm,

like my heart
turning now,
as darkness takes you,

and somewhere
a door slams,
long, long into the night.

# The Shape of Things

You gather-in mood, tone, a look,
working over the words,
as if a good pummelling ever made
better sense of anything.
Wrung out, hung up, the shape of things
is blindingly, dully, different.

Between even the oldest friends
Doubt hoists its tattered flag
and tiny moments blow away,
are slapped around in storm:
you have to tear it down, or wait
and trust for days of stillness, happiness.

## Ice

At Richmond the ice is crooning
under the tentative weight of sticks and pebbles
we lob and slide across a frozen pond. A marvel.

Strangers exchange troubled smiles,
never dreaming before that ice had its own song,
a dull forgiving echo for those who stand at the side

watching for cracks, those who don't know how to skate,
and those who try to read the hieroglyphs
under the soft muzz of scurf the dancers' heels kick up.

## Walking

*(for Miroslav Mandić and Jo Shapcott)*


Miroslav Mandić is walking.
From Hölderlin to Rimbaud he journeys
with solitude, a walking stick, sweat.
*It was the walking stick and me walking,*
*the two of us like waves.*
*It was the walking stick and me walking,*
*homelessness and I.*
In villages where they don't know
what poetry is, what art is, he explains
his walking, he explains poetry:
he tells them it is like love,
he tells them it is sweat.
I read his work in clumsy translation,
*the road opened me*, he writes.
Can he mean that? Just that? Yes.

Miroslav Mandić is walking
from Rimbaud to Blake, not to honour their work,
not because they are important but to celebrate
poetry. Sometimes wind blows colder than rain,
sometimes milk curdles in his knapsack,
but it is nothing, none of it matters,
and it is everything. *Isn't language also walking?*
*Isn't walking also a form of writing?*
*Isn't the road the greatest, the most beautiful*
*building in the world?*

Miroslav Mandić is walking.
At Bunhill Fields, near Blake's grave,
on London grass, his walking stick
becomes a huge pen, forms the word *i*,
in his country this means *and*.
And each footfall is an and, and each footfall
a small connecting word, a conjunctive,
a continuance, and, and, and.
He walks in order to turn every there into here
and he tells us it is like love,
he tells us it is sweat,
he tells us it is poetry, and

62